YEAR 6

Comparing Fiction Genres

KARINA LAW

Teachers' Resource for Guided Reading

A & C Black • London

Contents

White Wolves Series Consultant: Sue Ellis, Centre for Literacy in Primary Education

First published 2008 by
A & C Black Publishers Ltd
38 Soho Square, London, W1D 3HB

www.acblack.com

Text copyright © 2008 Karina Law
Illustrations copyright © 2008 Mark Oldroyd

The right of Karina Law to be identified as author and the right of Mark Oldroyd to be identified as the illustrator of this work have been asserted by them in accordance with the Copyrights, Designs and Patents Act 1988.

ISBN 978-1-4081-0078-3

A CIP catalogue for this book is available from the British Library.

This book is produced using paper that is made from wood grown in managed, sustainable forests. It is natural, renewable and recyclable. The logging and manufacturing processes conform to the environmental regulations of the country of origin.
Printed in Great Britain by Martins the Printers, Berwick upon Tweed.

Introduction

What is Guided Reading?

Guided Reading is a valuable part of literacy work in the classroom, helping children develop as active and independent readers who are able to engage with a text. The teacher works with a small group of about six children of similar reading ability, on an unfamiliar text that has been selected to offer a sufficient challenge but not to be in any way discouraging. The session will include a combination of silent reading, reading aloud and discussion of the text.

Aims of Guided Reading

The main aim of Guided Reading is to help children become fluent and independent readers. With the close observation and targeted support that working with a small group facilitates, the teacher can help the children to:
- read accurately and with appropriate expression;
- develop strategies for increasing understanding at all levels, including prediction, inference and deduction, through discussion and appropriate question/answer sessions;
- develop their personal response to texts;
- develop their enjoyment of reading.

How to organise Guided Reading

Ideally, each group will have one session of Guided Reading per week. Other children in the class can work on a variety of independent tasks, such as:
- working on a follow-up activity to a previous Guided Reading session;
- reading on in preparation for the next Guided Reading session;
- reading a book of their own choice;
- working with a Teaching Assistant or parent to have extra reading practice and support as necessary;
- recording a personal response in their reading journal.

The teacher can then focus fully on the Guided Reading group for that day.

The children will find it reassuring if the Guided Reading sessions follow a broadly similar structure each time. The teaching sequences in this guide will help ensure this, as well as offering suggestions for drawing the most out of each text.

Assessment

The small group work in Guided Reading offers an ideal opportunity for checking the reading strategies each child is using and where further support is needed. A brief note of each child's performance during a session can be made on the record card on p. 42 and will keep an ongoing record of progression.

How to Use This Book

Teaching sequences

This guide provides five teaching sequences to support the use of the three Year 6 short story anthologies containing fiction from different genres with a Guided Reading group. The books are:

Shadow Puppet and other ghost stories
Space Pirates and other sci-fi stories
Dark Eagle and other historical stories

Each book contains four short stories, one for less experienced readers, two for independent readers and one for more experienced readers. Each teaching sequence relates to one of the stories in the book and follows a similar format, as detailed below. There is also a general teaching sequence for each reading level, which can be used to compare the different fiction genres covered in the three anthologies.

The activities are suggestions for how to help children take the most out of each text and you will need to select from them depending on the needs of the individual children within the group.

Introduction

This includes ideas for starting the session by discussing what the children think the story will be about and other clues contained in the title.

Independent reading

Each Guided Reading session should include some silent reading and some reading aloud, though at this age and stage the proportion of reading aloud is likely to be greater with less experienced readers in order that you can assess each child's progress and offer support as necessary. What is essential is that the emphasis is on children's understanding and inferential reading.

Returning to the text

The initial questions in this section are designed to check children's understanding of key themes and events, particularly where a lack of understanding would inhibit appreciation of later sections of the text. Encourage children to support their answers by finding examples in the text.

Subsequent ideas for discussion or activities can be selected according to the requirements of the group you are working with. They include:

- discussion of themes and characters;
- discussion points to help children develop their higher order reading skills;
- ideas for widening the context so that children can relate a theme or event to their own experience;
- suggestions for drama activities.

Next steps

The activity sheets can be used for independent work in the classroom or for homework. They provide an opportunity for children to demonstrate their understanding of events, themes or characters, or for them to use their imagination. They are all an extension of one or more of the earlier suggestions for discussion.

Target Statements for Reading

The NLS target statements for reading at Year 6 will help inform your planning for progression in reading.

Speaking:

- Use a range of oral techniques to present persuasive arguments and engaging narratives
- Participate in whole-class debate using the conventions and language of debate, including standard English
- Use the techniques of dialogic talk to explore ideas, topics or issues

Group discussion and interaction:

- Consider examples of conflict and resolution, exploring the language used
- Understand and use a variety of ways to criticise constructively and respond to criticism

Word structure and spelling:

- Spell familiar words correctly and employ a range of strategies to spell difficult and unfamiliar words
- Use a range of appropriate strategies to edit, proofread and correct spelling in their own work, on paper and on screen

Understanding and interpreting texts:

- Appraise a text quickly, deciding on its value, quality or usefulness
- Understand underlying themes, causes and points of view
- Understand how writers use different structures to create coherence and impact
- Explore how word meanings change when used in different contexts
- Recognise rhetorical devices used to argue, persuade, mislead and sway the reader

Creating and shaping texts:

- Set their own challenges to extend achievement and experience in writing
- Use different narrative techniques to engage and entertain the reader
- In non-narrative, establish, balance and maintain viewpoints
- Select words and language drawing on their knowledge of literary features and formal and informal writing
- Integrate words, images and sounds imaginatively for different purposes

Drama:

- Improvise using a range of drama strategies and conventions to explore themes such as hopes, fears and desires
- Devise a performance considering how to adapt the performance for a specific audience
- Consider the overall impact of a live or recorded performance, identifying dramatic ways of conveying characters' ideas and building tension

Shadow Puppet and other ghost stories by *Jane Clarke*

Story Summaries

A Special Sort of Cat [less experienced reader]

A Special Sort of Cat is a ghost story that explores the different ways in which a family comes to terms with bereavement.

Soon after his father's funeral, four-year-old Jack announces that he has a cat. The cat, Mina, has appeared from nowhere. Jack learned her name from a "nice lady". Mina always seems to be around when the family need her, but mysteriously disappears when visitors come to the house.

On the first anniversary of Dad's death, the family visit his grave and, as they say their goodbyes, the "nice lady" appears with flowers for her father's grave. The mystery surrounding the "nice lady" deepens when it transpires that her father has been dead for over a century. It seems that Mina is a very special cat after all.

Seekers [Independent reader]

Seekers is a ghost story with a time-travel element. Ben's sister, Vicky, is celebrating her sixth birthday with a group of friends and Ben has been persuaded to play hide and seek with them. Vicky suggests that they hide in a cupboard under the stairs. After a short time, she decides to go and find her friends. Ben waits longer and when he finally leaves the cupboard he realises something strange has happened. The grandfather clock in the hall strikes four o'clock for a second time. As he explores the house, he discovers that he has travelled back in time. He encounters four little girls in long dresses, but they are not his sister's friends. He can see right through one of them – he is looking at a ghost! Frantically he searches for his sister, worried that she, too, may have turned into a ghost, but finds her fast asleep in the cupboard under the stairs. When Ben leaves the cupboard, it is as if he has never been away.

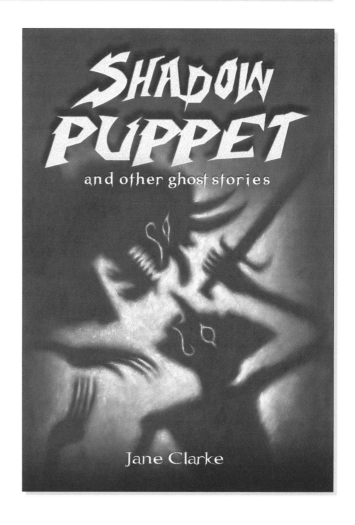

Shadow Puppet [Independent reader]

Shadow Puppet is a spooky tale about a boy who finds he is no longer in control of his actions. Sajil knows the difference between right and wrong and would never usually cheat or steal or hurt another person intentionally. So what is the reason for his new behaviour? When he notices that his shadow appears to have grown devilish horns, talons and claws, Sajil wonders if he is going mad. When he goes home, he discovers he has inherited a pair of Indonesian puppets from his great-auntie, and he devises a plan; if he can get the good prince puppet to defeat the ogre puppet, he may be able to retake control of his shadow. His plan doesn't quite work out as the puppet fight ends in a draw. Sajil tries to tear the head off the ogre puppet in desperation, which makes his mother take the puppets away and seal them inside a box. Sajil is delighted to find that everything returns to normal – at least as long as the puppets stay inside the box!

Smelling of Roses [More experienced reader]

Smelling of Roses interweaves past and present through the stories of two girls called Rose. The stories share the same setting but are 'told' at different times in history.

The present-day story opens with Rose climbing a hill to reach her school. She is suffering from asthma and, possibly, hay fever. We learn that her best friend is not speaking to her because she is cross that Rose went to a birthday party without her.

The other story describes the journey of Rose of the past as she descends the hill to work at the cotton mill. She is pregnant and living under a cloud of shame. Rose's best friend stopped speaking to her when she learned that Rose was pregnant.

The two stories overlap when present-day Rose makes her way down the hill and is overcome by the putrid smell of mildewed roses. At the same time, Rose of the past is trying to climb the hill in search of clean air. Halfway up the hill, she heads towards a thicket of roses where she decides to wait for someone to help her up the stepping stones. Present-day Rose reaches out for a pink rose. As she does so, its petals crumble and her lungs seem to fill with dust.

"I don't know how we'd have got through the last year without Mina," Mum was saying, "but we always knew she was someone else's cat." She smiled at me and Jack. "I'm looking forward to having a cat of our very own, aren't you?"

"You bet," Jack bounced along between us. "I like cats."

I emptied my mind of all the unasked and unanswerable questions.

"Dad would be happy for us, too," I laughed, as Mum and I swung Jack off his feet. "He liked cats."

22

Seekers

23

A Special Sort of Cat:
Teaching Sequence 1

Teaching Sequence

Introduction

How many of the children have read a ghost story before? Ask them to tell the group about the stories they have read. Explain that, as well as being a ghost story, this story also explores the different ways in which a family deals with losing a loved one.

Independent reading

Ask the group to read aloud the story, focusing on reading for meaning.

- Discuss less familiar words and phrases such as *twilight* (p. 11), *dunked*, *indignantly* (p. 14), *solemnly*, *scudding*, *headstone* (p. 17), *chrysanthemums* (p. 18), *tottered* (p. 19), *transfixed*, *gravestone*, *century*, *inscription* (p. 21).
- Discuss some of the informal expressions used and check that the children understand their meaning. For example, "as quiet as the grave"; "Jack piped up" (p. 9).
- Talk about the language play in *purr-fect* (p. 12).

Returning to the text

Develop children's understanding by asking some of these questions either during reading or at the end of the story. Encourage them to find the relevant part in the text to support their answers.

1) Which words and phrases in the first few pages tell us how much Jack's family are missing their dad? (For example, "my voice wobbled", "I missed him so much that it hurt" (p. 9), "my fake-cheerful voice" (p. 10), "my aching heart" (p. 11).)

2) What things remind Jack's family of Dad? (For example, his coat, the smell of his aftershave (p. 9), his favourite shirt (p. 12), his birthday (p. 15).)

3) "Life gradually began to return to a different sort of normal" (p. 15); what does the narrator mean by this? (Although life will never be the same for the family as it was before Dad died, they will start to settle into a new routine and life will begin to feel normal in a different way.)

Talk about the effect of the simile in the opening paragraph: "the house was as quiet as the grave" (p. 9). Discuss how, in addition to informing the reader of how silent the house feels without Dad, the author has used an image that is in keeping with the theme of death. The image also helps to establish that this is a ghost story.

Discuss the effect of the description of Mina on p. 10: "shadowy blue-grey". "Shadowy" is in keeping with the ghostly nature of the story; it also echoes the idea that the cat behaves like a shadow in the way she follows Jack around.

Talk about the awkwardness that the narrator feels with the family's friends (p. 13). In what way did Mina help? Explain how, often, people don't know what to say to someone who has lost a loved one, perhaps because they are afraid of saying the wrong thing. Having a cat there helps by giving them something else to talk about.

The "ghost" element of this story is quite subtle. Ask the group to talk about the features that set it apart from other stories, for example, the mysterious cat that appears and disappears without explanation; the birthday cake candles that mysteriously relight themselves; the mysterious "nice lady".

Next steps

The children can now complete Activity Sheet 1: "Mina", which asks them to find words and phrases in the story to describe the mysterious cat.

Mina

Find words and phrases in the story to describe Mina, the mysterious cat that visited Jack and his family when they needed her.

The way Jack describes Mina

_____

_____

_____

_____

Mina's appearance

_____

_____

_____

_____

The way Mina moves

_____

_____

_____

_____

The way Mina behaves

_____

_____

_____

_____

_____

White Wolves Teachers' Resource
for Guided Reading Year 6
Comparing Fiction Genres
© A & C Black 2008

Seekers: Teaching Sequence 2

Teaching Sequence

Introduction

How many of the children have read a ghost story before? Ask them to tell the group about the stories they have read. Discuss the title of this story; can the group guess the game that it refers to?

Independent reading

Ask the group to read aloud the story, focusing on reading for meaning.

- Discuss less familiar words and phrases such as *tiaras* (p. 25), *Reggae Boyz* (p. 26), *petticoats* (p. 27), *musty, odour* (p. 29), *wispier* (p. 31), *strode* (p. 32), *Aga* (p. 33), *stomach, somersault* (p. 34), *stammered, draught* (p. 35), *frantically* (p. 36), *shimmered* (p. 37), *wonderment* (p. 38).
- Talk about the meaning of the phrase "the girl stopped dead" (p. 34) and discuss what makes this particularly effective in a ghost story.

Returning to the text

Develop children's understanding by asking some of these questions either during reading or at the end of the story. Encourage them to find the relevant part in the text to support their answers.

1) What is unusual about the grandfather clock? (It strikes four o'clock three times during the afternoon (pp. 27, 30, 36).)
2) What makes Ben realise that the girls are not his sister's friends? (They shout for Victoria; Ben's sister, Vicky, hates being called by her full name (p. 32).)
3) What physical changes happen to Ben, showing that he felt afraid? (The hairs on his arms stood on end (p. 31), he shuddered (p. 34), the blood drained from his face (p. 35).)
5) After the ghost girls have "dissolved into nothingness" (p. 36), Ben searches the house frantically for his sister. What is he afraid may have happened to her? (He worries that she may have become a ghost (p. 37).)

Discuss how the opening pages describe an ordinary family celebration and there is nothing to suggest that this is a ghost story. Notice how the tone begins to change on p. 27. For example, the reference to the cupboard under the stairs with the creaky door and the cobweb that Ben brushes against.

Reread the scene in which Ben tries to scare Vicky (p. 29). How does the author build tension? Note the musty smell, the cold and the cobwebs, and our first encounter with the word "ghost". Ironically, it is Ben who mentions it and he only does so to scare his sister and liven up the game.

Discuss the unusual appearance of the ghost girls and ask the group to find references that signal to Ben that they are ghosts. (For example, their dresses seemed greyer and wispier (p. 31), Ben is able to see through them, they have "mirror eyes" (p. 35), they "dissolved into nothingness" (p. 36).)

Look at how the author has included humour in this ghost story. Vicky and her friends find lots to giggle about and Ben has a good sense of fun, for example, he enjoys trying to scare his sister (p. 29). At the end of the story the author gives the last laugh to Mum who asks Ben, "you'd love to play another game of hide and seek with your sister, wouldn't you?" (p. 39). Although we don't know his reply, we can imagine the look on Ben's face!

Ask two children to role-play the characters of Ben and Vicky. Other children could ask them questions about the birthday party to explore their different perspectives on the day's events.

Next steps

Children can imagine they are Ben and write a diary account of the day's events using Activity Sheet 2: "The Cupboard Under the Stairs".

The Cupboard Under the Stairs

Imagine you are Ben, and write a diary account of the day's events.

- Describe how different the house looked when you travelled back in time.

- What did you think when you heard the grandfather clock strike four o'clock again?

- How did you feel when you saw a little girl in a long, silver-grey dress and you realised she was a ghost.

_____

_____

_____

_____

_____

_____

_____

_____

_____

_____

_____

_____

_____

White Wolves Teachers' Resource
for Guided Reading Year 6
Comparing Fiction Genres
© A & C Black 2008

Shadow Puppet: Teaching Sequence 3

Teaching Sequence

Introduction

How many of the children have read a ghost story before? Ask them to tell the group about the stories they have read.

If possible, show the children a clip of a shadow puppet show to demonstrate how light and silhouettes can be used to create a dramatic effect.

Independent reading

Ask the group to read aloud the story, focusing on reading for meaning.

- Discuss less familiar words and phrases such as *chipped*, *elongated* (p. 43), *spindly* (p. 44), *Indonesia* (p. 45), *projecting*, *stifled* (p. 47), *menacingly*, *devilish* (p. 50), *chiselled*, *traditional robes* (p. 52), *evilly*, *bulbous*, *ogre* (p. 53), *hideous* (p. 54), *grimaced*, *projected*, *engulf* (p. 55), *epic*, *ghastly*, *heritage* (p. 57).

- Talk about the informal expressions, for example, "The hairs on the back of Sajil's neck prickled" (p. 53), "Sajil's heart was in his mouth" (p. 56).

Returning to the text

Develop children's understanding by asking some of these questions either during reading or at the end of the story. Encourage them to find the relevant part in the text to support their answers.

1) At what point does the tone become sinister? (For example, when Ryan watches open-mouthed as his shadow pushes Ryan's shadow away (p. 44).

2) In this story, Sajil behaves aggressively, cheats and steals. How do we know that this is not the way he usually behaves? (For example, "He never copied!" (p. 47); he is horrified when he sees the empty chocolate wrapper in his hands and returns to the shop to pay for it (p. 48).)

3) On p. 47, Sajil is alarmed to discover that his shadow has grown horns. What other strange and disturbing things does he notice about his

shadow? (For example, "claw-like fingers" (p. 48), "taloned feet" (p. 49), "devilish grin", "pointed fangs" (p. 50).)

4) Sajil's mum is delighted when the shadow puppet fight ends in a draw but Sajil declares, "I don't like draws" (p. 56). At what other time has he said something similar? (At the start of the story Sajil is unhappy when his football team draws with the Hackford Hawks (p. 46).)

Talk about the strong opening to this story; do the group like the way the author jumps straight into the action? Note how *Shadow Puppet* begins and ends with a scene on the football pitch, giving the story a symmetry. The battles on the football pitch also provide a parallel with the battle between good and evil acted out by the shadow puppets.

Compare the descriptions of the Prince of Goodness and Light (p. 52) and the figure of the ogre (p. 53) and Mum's reaction to each; note the antonyms used (darkness / light; goodness / wickedness). Talk about the simile on p. 55: "as hunched and menacing as a watchful vulture"; ask the children to think about what makes this description so effective. Ask them to experiment with other similes using adjectives from the text, for example, "as hideous as…", "as ghastly as…".

Draw the group's attention to the text on pp. 53–54; discuss how this is the pivotal point in the story; Mum explains that, in the fight between good and evil, the outcome depends on who is in control; Mum is referring to the puppets, but Sajil recognises her words may hold the key to how he can defeat the evil force that seems to have taken over his shadow.

Next steps

Using Activity Sheet 3: "What Would You Do?" children can write a sequel to *Shadow Puppet*, imagining they are Sajil on his 18th birthday.

What Would You Do?

Imagine you are Sajil and your 18th birthday is approaching. Write a sequel to *Shadow Puppet* explaining what you would do about the unwanted heirloom taped inside the box on top of your mother's wardrobe? Refer back to the story for inspiration when writing descriptions of the shadow puppets and the battle between good and evil that they represent.

Life's been pretty good since the day Mum packed those ghastly puppets away. Even my team are doing well in the League! Mum didn't realise she was doing me a favour. Sometimes I think I must have imagined it all. A silly toy can't really be responsible for all the strange things that happened to me back then. Can it? I suppose I'll find out in a day or two…

_____

_____

_____

_____

_____

_____

_____

_____

_____

_____

_____

_____

_____

White Wolves Teachers' Resource
for Guided Reading Year 6
Comparing Fiction Genres
© A & C Black 2008

Smelling of Roses: Teaching Sequence 4

Teaching Sequence

Introduction

How many of the children have read a ghost story before? Ask them to tell the group about the stories they have read.

Explain that part of this story is set in the past and focuses on a girl who works in a cotton mill. What do the group know about this industry?

Independent reading

Ask the group to read aloud the story, focusing on reading for meaning.

- Discuss less familiar words and phrases such as *vaguely, horrendous* (p. 61), *asthma inhaler* (p. 63), *dock her pay, outhouse, billowed, nausea* (p. 64), *clogs odour* (p. 65), *fragrance* (p. 66), *fusty, mildew* (p. 67), *racking cough, Industrial Revolution* (p. 68), *gagging* (p. 70), *mechanics, seductively* (p. 71), *courage* (p. 72), *vaguely* (p. 73), *retched, suffocate, trudging, putrid, forearms* (p. 74).
- Check that the children understand the expression, "Another day at t'mill" (p. 63).

Returning to the text

Develop children's understanding by asking some of these questions either during reading or at the end of the story. Encourage them to find the relevant part in the text to support their answers.

1) The central characters in this story are following the same path. Where are they heading? (One is descending the hill to work at the cotton mill; the other is climbing the hill to reach her school at the top.)
2) Why are the characters struggling to reach their destinations? (The character descending the hill is pregnant and is feeling sick (p. 64); The other chacter is carrying a heavy backpack and suffering from asthma (pp. 62 and 63).)

Discuss the way this story is told. There are two voices, both telling a story in the same setting but at different times in history. The story set in the present day is written as a "first-person" account and narrated in the present tense; the story set in italics is written in the "third person" and narrated in the past tense.

Discuss the poetic style of the prose set in italics, including the use of alliteration and metaphor. Ask the children to identify lines that are particularly effective. For example, "While the noisy machines were silenced, beneath the shroud of smoke, the cool, dank air came alive with gossip"; "a tangle of wild roses was blooming in a patch of smoky sunlight", "The plump, red rosehips looked ripe and tempting, good enough to eat" (p. 71).

Draw the group's attention to the phrase, "I'm lost in time" (p.69); what is the significance of this statement? (By the end of the story, Rose does become caught between past and present.)

Talk about the author's use of scent and smell in this story. Ask the group to find powerful descriptions and talk about their effect on the reader. In particular, look at the way the author describes the smell of the roses. Notice how the description changes, reflecting the tone of the story at different times. For example, "The whole path smells of roses. Putrid, mildewed roses." (p. 74) and "They look gorgeous, and their scent is just heavenly." (p. 75).

Talk about the ending of the story. How do the children interpret it? Might there be a number of different ways to interpret the ending?

Next steps

Using Activity Sheet 4: "Rose Thorns", children can write a diary entry for Rose from the cotton mill. Remind them they should write or tell her story in the first person.

Rose Thorns

Write a diary entry for Rose describing what life is like working at the cotton mill and how it feels to be alone, homeless and expecting a baby.

I was nearly late for work this morning. If I lose this job, I don't know what I shall do. I'd never be able to feed myself, let alone the baby I'm carrying inside me. My best friend still isn't speaking to me...

_____

_____

_____

_____

_____

_____

_____

_____

_____

_____

_____

_____

_____

_____

White Wolves Teachers' Resource
for Guided Reading Year 6
Comparing Fiction Genres
© A & C Black 2008

Space Pirates and other sci-fi stories
by *Tony Bradman*

Story Summaries

Alien Invasion! [less experienced reader]
This is a humorous, science-fiction story with a familiar setting. Megan's dad can't sleep because her hamster, Harry, thunders around on his exercise wheel all night. The next night, Megan is woken by a noise, but Harry is not to blame. The family head down to the garden to investigate. Something makes Megan throw a cover over her hamster's cage and take him with her. Outside, the source of the strange noise is revealed as a flying saucer lands on the garden shed. Things take a sinister turn when five terrifying figures emerge carrying weapons. When Dad tells the alien leader to calm down, the aliens point their weapons at the family causing Mum to scream and pull the children towards her. The cover slips off the cage, revealing Harry the hamster. When the aliens see Harry, they become frightened; it transpires they worship hamsters as gods. Megan seizes the opportunity, telling the aliens that the Great God Harry the Hamster is very angry and he wants them to leave his planet immediately. The aliens obey instantly, pausing only to restore the flattened shed with a beam of silver light.

This is Not Earth [independent reader]
This is not Earth, as the title suggests, is set on another planet: K1754. Earth has been destroyed by war and pollution. For most of his life, Jamie had lived on a crowded starship with stale air, unappetizing food and very little privacy. Like many others, Jamie had caught Space Fever, which, although it hadn't killed him, has left him with painful sores. Then Jamie is taken to Planet K1754, and life improves dramatically. Jamie loves the freedom that it offers. But Jamie's parents know that they cannot stay there because they are unable to grow crops and soon they will run out

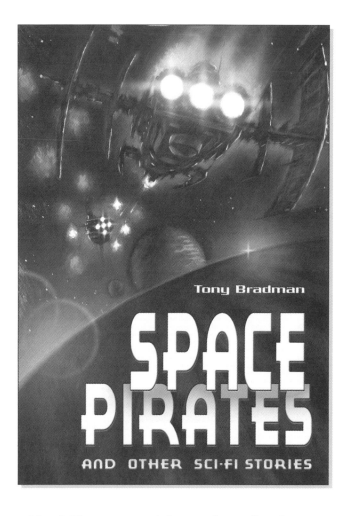

of food. The captain of the starship will only give them supplies if they can give him something in return. Jamie is so unhappy about leaving that he runs away. But then he discovers a cluster of unusual plants growing at the side of a pond. As he investigates, a leaf brushes against his hand and cures the Space Fever sore almost instantly. Jamie realises the importance of his discovery and rushes back to his parents with the good news. At last the family have something to trade in return for more supplies, and they can stay on Planet K1754.

Space Pirates [independent reader]
Kyle Raker, his dad, and Gizmo their dog, have gone on a day trip to planet Rigel 3 in their spaceship, the *Happy Rakers*. Dad is a trader, but

business has not been good and it doesn't look like Kyle's going to get his promised trip to World of Fun, the coolest theme-park planet in 500 star systems. Dad returns to the spaceship in a hurry to leave, and soon afterwards they are being shot at. Tarkel the Vile, the second most notorious pirate in the galaxy after Ogron the Unspeakable, is following them. Kyle's dad has discovered his hideout and is planning to steal Tarkel's treasure and then inform the Space Police of the location. His plan does not work out as Tarkel forces his way on to the *Happy Rakers*. However, Kyle manages to dissuade him from shooting by offering to provide him with the location of Ogron's treasure. Tarkel agrees and, once he is safely out of the way, Kyle reveals that he has a record of the co-ordinates to Tarkel's hideout and suggests they give the information to the Space Police. There might even be a reward at the end of it all. Enough, perhaps, for three tickets to World of Fun!

Everything I Need [More experienced reader]

Everything I Need is set in an imaginary future, in war-torn London. The story focuses on an isolated, desperate boy whose parents and sister were killed by looters during "The Bad Time". Now he has to manage alone with just his dog, Alfie, for company. Then he meets Eve, a girl his own age, who offers him food and friendship. The boy has made a rule for himself to "steer clear of people" but he notices that Alfie has taken a liking to her, so he follows her into the basement of what was once a bookshop. He gratefully accepts the food she offers him and listens to her story. But Eve awakens painful memories in him and this strengthens his resolve not to make friends with her in case she should die or turn out to be mad or horrible after all. He walks away from the girl, but something makes him go back. Eve is still in the basement when he returns and she welcomes him with a look of pleasure. He asks for more food, which she gives him on the condition he tells her his name: it is Adam.

a course for the nearest Space Police station and give them the co-ordinates to Tarkel's hideout…"

"But we don't have them," said Dad. "He deleted our files."

"No, he didn't, Dad," said Kyle with a sigh. "The computer's got a back-up facility, remember? I put it in for you last year."

"Oh, right," said Dad, and smiled. "Hey, maybe there's a reward for information about Tarkel – enough for three tickets to World of Fun." His smile vanished. "But if there is, I'll have to explain all this to your mum. You will help me come up with a good story, won't you?"

"Sure, Dad, absolutely *no* problem," said Kyle, taking his seat again and punching a new course into the control panel. "That's a promise."

EVERYTHING I NEED

59

58

Alien Invasion!: Teaching Sequence 1

Teaching Sequence

Introduction
Talk about the title and ask the group to discuss what sort of story it is likely to be and where they think it might be set.

Independent reading
Ask the group to read aloud the story, focusing on reading for meaning.
- Discuss less familiar words and phrases such as *Darth Vader* (p. 7), *pensioner* (p. 8), *frantic, hectic, meteorites* (p. 9), *tongue* (p. 10), *hind, obviously, volume* (p. 11), *metallic, awestruck, close encounter* (p. 13) *occupants, advanced, huddle* (p. 15), *surrender, Earthlings, "Krell", resist, utterly, aggressive, threatening, fleet, orbit* (p. 16), *invasion fleet* (p. 17), *deception* (p. 19).

Returning to the text
Develop children's understanding by asking some of these questions either during reading or at the end of the story. Encourage them to find the relevant part in the text to support their answers.
1) What was keeping Dad awake? (To begin with, it was Megan's hamster, Harry, in his exercise wheel (p. 7); later, it is a "deep, throbbing sound" coming from the garden (p. 11).
2) At what point does the tone of the story change? (Mum becomes anxious when the hatch to the saucer begins to open (p. 14) and things take a sinister turn when five terrifying figures emerge carrying weapons and threatening the family (pp. 15–16).)
3) How do the aliens behave when they see Megan's hamster? (Their behaviour is no longer aggressive and bullying; they show fear and humility; they appear to worship the hamster (pp. 17–18).)

Discuss the way in which the author plays a trick on the reader at the start of the story: "Megan slowly opened her eyes and stared at the strange creature in her bedroom doorway..." (p. 7). What were the children's first thoughts when they read this line?

Talk about the humorous nature of the story and ask the group to identify the lines that they found funniest. For example, when the flying saucer crushes the garden shed on landing, Mum says to Dad: "Whoops... They park just like you, dear." (p. 14). Touches like this remind the reader of the familiar setting; the story successfully contrasts ordinary family life with an extraordinary sci-fi theme.

Discuss the ways in which the author concludes this light-hearted story with a happy ending. The alien bullies are outwitted, Megan enjoys a new-found respect from the other family members, Harry the hamster no longer faces the threat of spending his nights in the shed, Dad decides to buy earplugs to help him sleep.

Hot-seat characters from the story in a role-play activity. Ask some members of the group to pretend to be Megan and her parents. Ask the rest to pretend to be reporters interviewing them for a television report about the strange event. Children could prepare for the activity by writing down a few questions before they begin. For example, "What did you think when you first saw the flying saucer?", "Were you afraid that the aliens might want to take you prisoner?", "Is it possible you might have imagined or dreamt the whole thing?"

Next steps
The children could write a "News Flash!" report for a local television studio using Activity Sheet 1. Ask them to include comments drawn from the interview with the family. If possible, give the children an opportunity to read out their reports to the class in the style of a news reporter.

News Flash!

Write a news report for a local television studio about the recent sighting of a flying saucer. Include eyewitness comments drawn from an interview with the family who claim to have seen the flying saucer and spoken to the group of aliens on board.

"Good evening, and welcome to the six o'clock news. Yesterday we reported that a giant cloud of meteorites had been detected heading towards Earth. Following that report, there have been some very interesting developments...

_____

_____

_____

_____

_____

_____

_____

_____

_____

_____

_____

This is Not Earth: Teaching Sequence 2

Teaching Sequence

Introduction
Talk about the title of this story. What sort of story is it likely to be and where do the group think it might be set?

Independent reading
Ask the group to read aloud the story, focusing on reading for meaning.
- Discuss less familiar words and phrases such as *voice activated* (p.23), *colossal* (p. 24), *humanity, pollution, Galileo, The Great Exodus, inedible, disputes* (p. 25), *permanent, colonise* (p. 26), *rodent, gene* (p. 27), *substitute, self-sufficient* (p. 28), *thriving,* (p.29), *ladling, atmosphere* (p. 30), *flimsy* (p. 31), *eerie* (p. 33), *clustered, intense* (p. 35).

Returning to the text
Develop children's understanding by asking some of these questions either during reading or at the end of the story. Encourage them to find the relevant part in the text to support their answers.
1) What details in the opening passages of this story support the idea expressed in the title, that *This is not Earth*? (For example, the pink sky and purple sand (p. 23).)
2) What does Jamie love about Planet K1754? (For example, the fresh air and wide open spaces (p. 26); it feels like the home he has always wanted (p. 27).)
3) Why do Jamie and his parents have to leave Planet K1754? (They cannot be self-sufficient there because they are unable to grow crops and make the farm work (pp. 28–29); if they stay, they will run out of food (p. 30).)
4) Why is Jamie so pleased about his discovery? (Firstly, it is a cure for Space Fever, which will bring relief to him and others; secondly, it means that his family has something to trade for supplies which means they will be able to continue living on Planet K1754.)

Talk about Jamie's unusual gadgets. For example, his hover-bike and voice-activated helmet radio (p. 23). If the children could employ Jamie's dad to build a space gadget for them, what would they ask for?

Reread the description of Jamie's planet on pp. 24–25. Does it sound like the sort of environment the group would like to live in or visit? Do they think it possible that planet Earth might one day be unsuitable for human inhabitants as a result of war and pollution? Do they think humans could live on another planet?

In addition to the gadgets and landscape, talk about the details that set this story in the sci-fi genre. For example, the *Galileo's* gene banks that provide Jamie's parents with frozen seeds to plant, in an attempt to grow wheat, vegetables and fruit (p. 27). Reread the descriptions of the family's living quarters on the *Galileo* (p. 25) and inside the dome (p. 28). The author has even invented a disease: Space Fever (pp. 25–26).

Discuss the reasons why Jamie decides to run away. What do the group think about his decision? How would his parents have felt?

In groups of three, children can act out a scene between Jamie and his parents, with Jamie begging them to let him continue living on the planet he loves, and Jamie's parents trying to explain the reasons why they cannot stay.

Next steps
The children could write a feature about "Planet K1754" for a travel brochure using Activity Sheet 2. Ask them to use persuasive language, promoting the planet as the perfect holiday destination.

Planet K1754

Write a feature about Planet K1754 for a travel brochure. Use persuasive language to promote the planet as the perfect holiday destination.

Planet K1754

From the moment you set foot on this beautiful planet, you won't be disappointed! The clean, crisp, fresh air, wide-open spaces and total sense of freedom make this the perfect holiday destination for travellers wanting to get away from it all!

_____

_____

_____

_____

_____

_____

_____

_____

_____

_____

TRAVEL FACT FILE	
Vaccinations required:	Tetanus, Polio, Space Fever
Distance from Earth:	
Climate:	
Currency:	

White Wolves Teachers' Resource
for Guided Reading Year 6
Comparing Fiction Genres
© A & C Black 2008

Space Pirates: Teaching Sequence 3

Teaching Sequence

Introduction

Talk about the title of this story. What sort of story is it likely to be and where do the group think it might be set?

Discuss the idea of a "space pirate". How might they differ from an ordinary pirate?

Independent reading

Ask the group to read aloud the story, focusing on reading for meaning.

- Discuss less familiar words and phrases such as *horizontally, tripod, freighter, vessel, cargo hold* (p. 41), *dominated, co-pilot, brooding, barren, dreary, sector, colony* (p. 42), *nebula, comet, astronomy, colossal* (p. 43), *agitated, pulsed* (p. 44), *G-force, distorted, asteroids* (p. 45), *co-ordinates* (p. 46), *exception, intrigued* (p. 47), *juddered, stern to tip, force field* (p. 48), *vile, notorious* (p. 49), *databank* (p. 50), *ominously* (p. 52), *Reptilian* (p. 54), *reprieve* (p. 56).

Returning to the text

Develop children's understanding by asking some of these questions either during reading or at the end of the story. Encourage them to find the relevant part in the text to support their answers.

1) Kyle's dad is said to "have a habit of getting involved in what could only be described as 'dodgy deals'…" (p. 44). What do you think this means?

2) When Kyle's dad returns to the spaceship, why is he in such a hurry to leave? (He has angered "Tarkel the Vile"; the second most notorious pirate in the galaxy (p. 49).)

3) How does Kyle outwit Tarkel? (He provides Tarkel with the location of Ogron's treasure. He wipes the co-ordinates of Tarkel's hideout from their computer in the knowledge that he has a back-up copy which he intends to give to the Space Police.)

Look at some of the space detail that the author has included to give a strong sense of the place for this sci-fi story. (For example, "They shot past Rigel 3's moon and the other planets in the system, several of which were enormous gas giants, and whizzed through a belt of ice-bound asteroids" (p. 45).) Ask the group to find other effective descriptions of the space setting.

Talk about the World of Fun: "the coolest theme-park planet in 500 star systems" (p. 42). How do the children think this theme park might differ from theme parks on planet Earth? What sort of rides and attractions do they think might be there?

Consider Kyle's dad's uncomfortable reaction when his son confronts him about whether his actions are legal: "'Er… I wouldn't go quite *that* far,' said Dad, avoiding Kyle's gaze." (p. 47). How might his "dodgy dealings" differ from the vile and unspeakable acts of the space pirates?

Discuss the space-pirate characters created by Tony Bradman. Ask the group to look for descriptions of these "vile" and "unspeakable" characters in the text. What does Tarkel look like (p. 54), and what do the group imagine he has done to earn his notorious reputation?

Ask the group what they think Kyle's mum would have to say when she found out what happened on the day trip to Rigel 3. Would Kyle and his father tell her exactly what happened? Children could explore their ideas through role-play, by acting out the scene.

Next steps

Using Activity Sheet 3: "Vile and Unspeakable", children can create a space pirate of their own and write a short story based on their character.

Vile and Unspeakable

Create a space pirate of your own: the *third* most notorious space pirate in the galaxy. Think about the following questions and then write a full description of their character.

- What name will you give your space pirate?
- What will they look like?
- What have they done to earn their notorious reputation?

_____

_____

_____

_____

_____

_____

_____

_____

_____

_____

_____

_____

_____

_____

White Wolves Teachers' Resource
for Guided Reading Year 6
Comparing Fiction Genres
© A & C Black 2008

Everything I Need: Teaching Sequence 4

Teaching Sequence

Introduction

Explain that this is a sci-fi story. Ask the group to talk about what this means and what features they expect to find in the story.

Independent reading

Ask the group to read aloud the story, focusing on reading for meaning.

- Discuss less familiar words and phrases such as *intact*, *pockmarked* (p. 62) *parka* (p. 63), *warily* (p. 64), *sheath*, *hilt* (p. 65), *illuminating*, *beacon* (p. 66), *oasis*, *plague*, *occupant*, *gas cylinder* (p. 67), *faltering*, *poise* (p. 68), *looters* (p. 70), *mingle* (p. 71).
- Talk about the author's use of colloquialisms and check that the group understand their meaning. For example, *get his bearings* (p. 61), *steer clear* (p. 64), *pickings*, *holed up* (p. 65), *chummy* (p. 68).

Returning to the text

Develop children's understanding by asking some of these questions either during reading or at the end of the story. Encourage them to find the relevant part in the text to support their answers.

1) Where and when is this story set? (London, in an imaginary future.)
2) What was "The Bad Time" (p. 61)? (Probably the time when Adam's parents and sister were killed by looters (pp. 69 and 70). However, Eve also uses this term (p. 71) so it could be a reference to the war.)
3) Why is Adam reluctant to make friends with the girl? (He had made a rule for himself to "steer clear of people" (p. 64); they were usually either "bad news" (p. 63) or "they were nice – and died" (p. 70).

The story slowly reveals details that tell us a war has taken place. Ask the group to locate some of them. For example: Adam's military style of clothing: combat trousers and heavy boots; a rusty, bombed-out tank (p. 61), the buildings that remain intact are "pockmarked with bullet holes (p. 62), food is scarce.

Discuss the ways in which *Everything I Need* differs from other stories with wartime settings. This is not an historical story; it is a science-fiction story with an imaginary, futuristic setting.

Discuss the theme of loneliness. Should the pair stick together as the girl suggests, or is Adam right to be wary of making a friendship with her? He tells her: "I don't want to get tied up with anyone, it just doesn't work. I've got everything I need" (p. 73). Notice how Adam's words allude back to the title of the story. The girl doesn't believe Adam. Discuss with the group whether *they* believe him. Adam worries about what might happen if he were to stay with Eve and they became friends but she got ill and died (p. 75). Is this a good enough reason for them *not* to become friends?

Talk about the characters' names: Adam and Eve; why might the author have used these names? Do they think he wants us to view the friendship between the characters as a new beginning? A sign of hope, perhaps? The final line suggests that the hostile world outside is waiting "for a future to begin" (p. 78).

Ask the children to imagine they have woken up to find themselves in the landscape that Tony Bradman has described in *Everything I Need*. Ask them to describe what they see, hear and feel to the group or to a partner. What would they do and what would they look for?

Next steps

Children can write a sequel to *Everything I Need* using Activity Sheet 4: "A New Beginning".

A New Beginning

Imagine that *Everything I Need* is the first chapter in a longer story. What do you think would happen next?
Begin a second chapter, continuing on a separate sheet if necessary.

_____

_____

_____

_____

_____

_____

_____

_____

_____

_____

_____

_____

_____

_____

_____

_____

_____

White Wolves Teachers' Resource
for Guided Reading Year 6
Comparing Fiction Genres
© A & C Black 2008

Dark Eagle and other historical stories by *Neil Tonge*

Story Summaries

The Sun God [less experienced reader]

The Sun God is set in Egypt during the reign of Tutankhamun. The story is narrated by Hamu, a twelve-year-old boy who devotes his life to his beloved master, the god-king of Egypt. Hamu came to court as cupbearer to Tutankhamun, working under the watchful eye of power-hungry Ay. Ay dislikes Hamu and is suspicious of his friendship with the king. One morning, Ay tells Hamu to place a powder in the king's drink. Hamu pretends to obey but later empties the cup, fearing that Ay is trying to poison the king. Despite Hamu's efforts, Tutankhamun is found dead a few days later and his body is prepared for burial in the customary way. Hamu decides to slip into his tomb with him and accept death, in the hope that when Ra, the Sun god comes to collect his master's soul, he will take Hamu, too.

Dark Eagle [independent reader]

Dark Eagle is a tale of conflict and divided loyalty, set in Roman Britain. Dubornos, the innkeeper, and the Brigantes warriors are planning to launch an attack on the Roman fort. Dubornos' nephew, Brean, is the only other person who knows about the plan. Dubornos' ill-treatment of his nephew proves to be his own downfall as Brean switches his loyalty to Centurion Marcus, who has shown him kindness and promised him employment as a soldier. Brean tells Centurion Marcus everything. Marcus takes ownership of the inn and throws Dubornos out, telling his soldiers to "rid us of him for ever". When Dubornos' friends return to the inn, they are met by Centurion Marcus. He brings both men to the ground and orders that they be thrown over the cliff. Finally, Marcus offers Brean the position of landlord and orders a bowl of fine, Flavian wine.

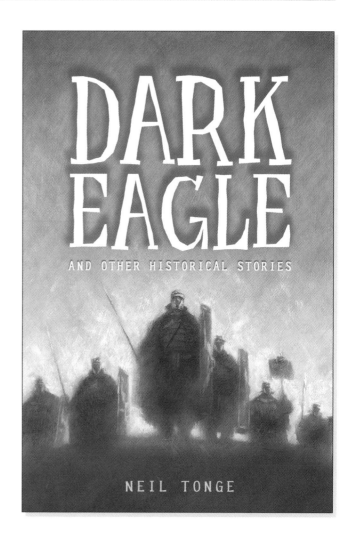

Escape from the Workhouse
[independent reader]

James and Anne are forced to enter the workhouse when their parents die of cholera. The workhouse is a frightening, hostile place and they are treated cruelly by all except their new friend, Tommy Ticky. Worst of all is the beadle, who runs the workhouse in military fashion, instilling harsh discipline and addressing the children as though they are vermin. They find life hard; they are starving most of the time and their fingers are raw from unpicking old sailing ropes day after day. Then the beadle announces that Anne is to go and work as a scullery girl in a big house and James decides it is time to act. When the beadle orders him and Anne to take a distressed Tommy Ticky back to his tower, he seizes the opportunity. James finds a trapdoor and the three children lower themselves down through the floor, from where they make their escape into the street. They flee the clutches of the beadle and head for the River Tyne, hopeful of a life of freedom.

Left Behind [More experienced reader]
It's 1940 and Len and his brother Reggie are travelling through France with other evacuees when their convoy of lorries is attacked German dive-bombers. The brothers tumble into a ditch and are separated from the rest of their group. They flee to the safety of the woods, where they are discovered by British soldiers who are fighting a running retreat from the Germans. One of the soldiers, Ernest Grisstock, is ordered to take the boys to the French coast so that they get back to Britain. The boys find themselves caught up in the crossfire before they make their escape in a motorcycle and sidecar. Ernest successfully gets the boys to Dunkirk, where he entrusts them to a group of wounded soldiers. The boys make it back to 'Blighty' but Ernest stays behind. Some time later, the brothers learn that Ernest was declared "missing in action, probably dead". They return to Dunkirk 60 years later and leave a wreath in honour of their rescuer.

towards a giant pair of balancing scales at the far end. Next to the scales, a god in the shape of a crocodile would be sitting. My master's heart would be plucked from his body and placed on the scales and weighed against a feather. If it was too heavy, then the crocodile would tear the king's body apart with his sharp teeth and swallow it.

But I know this will not happen. Tutankhamun's heart is pure and he will be saved. My master was a good man. He was kind to me, his cupbearer.

A day or perhaps two days have passed. There's little air to breathe now. The reed light has gone out and I am surrounded by darkness. I make a pillow with my arms and rest my head. My eyes close and as I fall asleep, I see a bright light which fills my head. It is Ra. He has come for us.

18

Dark Eagle

19

The Sun God: Teaching Sequence 1

Teaching Sequence

Introduction

Explain that this story is set in ancient Egypt. Ask the children to tell you briefly what they know about this culture. If possible, show them pictures or video clips of characters and settings that feature in the story, for example, the mask of Tutankhamun, the tomb of Tutankhamun, the River Nile, the Valley of the Kings.

Independent reading

Ask the group to read aloud the story, focusing on reading for meaning.

- Discuss any less familiar words and phrases such as *tomb, flickering, cupbearer* (p. 7), *nobles* (p. 8), *utter* (p. 10), *Pharaoh, worthy* (p. 11), *pierced* (p. 12), *bedchamber, threatening, afterworld* (p. 13), *blurted, stomach, organs, nostrils* (p. 14), *courtyard, procession* (p. 16), *soul* (p. 17).
- Check that children understand the expression, "Stay your hand" (p. 10).
- Help with the pronunciation of character and place names such as *Tutankhamun, Hamu, Harum* (p. 7), *Syrians* (p. 9).

Returning to the text

Develop children's understanding by asking some of these questions either during reading or at the end of the story. Encourage them to find the relevant part in the text to support their answers.

1) What did Hamu's work as cupbearer involve? (He made sure that if the king wanted wine, it would always be ready for him (p. 7).)
2) Why do you think Ay hated Tutankhamun?
3) Tutankhamun told Hamu that he would love to exchange places with him, even if it was for just one day (p. 11); why do you think he felt this way?
4) The king was found on the floor of his bedchamber with a fatal head wound (p. 13). What do you think happened to him?

5) Why were the king's possessions and furniture placed in the tomb with him? (The Egyptians believed the king would need them for a new life in the next world (p. 17).)

Talk about the way in which the king's body is prepared for burial (pp. 14–16). Discuss how this scene gives us a sense of ancient Egyptian culture. This is a key aspect of historical fiction writing. As well as telling an interesting tale, the author is teaching us a little about what life was like during the reign of Tutankhamun; fact and fiction are interwoven.

Discuss Hamu's actions at the end of the story. What was his motivation for joining his master in the tomb, even though he knew that this meant he would die, too? Was it an act of courage or foolishness? What sort of life would he have faced had he not chosen this course of action? In the final paragraph (p. 18), does Hamu seem fearful, or at peace with the decision he has made?

How do the group imagine Tuthankhamun's people would have felt at the loss of their king? What sort of future would they be facing with Ay as their pharaoh?

Children could act out a scene similar to the one on p.10, when Hamu accidentally spilt wine at the king's feet. They could work in groups of three with one child playing Hamu, one child playing Ay and the other playing the boy-king. Ask the group to think about how the king will respond.

Next steps

The children could write a news report for an ancient Eygptian newspaper, using Activity Sheet 1: "The King is Dead!" Ask them to write an account of the events outlined in the story and remind them that, as a journalist, their viewpoint would be different from that of Hamu's.

The King is Dead!

Write a news report describing the events surrounding the death of the god-king, Tutankhamun.

- Describe how the dead king was found.
- Include an eyewitness quote from the maid who discovered the king's body.
- Write what people thought of their king.
- Describe what sort of ceremony will take place when the king is buried.

The Daily Tut

The king is dead!

Story continues page 2

White Wolves Teachers' Resource
for Guided Reading Year 6
Comparing Fiction Genres
© A & C Black 2008

Dark Eagle: Teaching Sequence 2

Teaching Sequence

Introduction

Explain that this story is set in Roman Britain. Ask the children to tell you briefly what they know about this period. If possible, show them pictures of Roman soldiers, centurions and places featured in the story, for example, Hadrian's Wall.

Independent reading

Ask the group to read aloud the story, focusing on reading for meaning.

- Discuss less familiar words and phrases such as *tunic* (p. 21), *swine, curse, legionaries* (p. 22), *tankards, cuff* (p. 23), *birch, patrol, slaughter, Centurion* (p. 24), *barrel-chested* (p. 25), *auxiliary regiment, tribesmen, plague, territory* (p. 26), *tribal, loyalty* (p. 27), *brewing, massacred* (p. 30), *deliberation, hilt* (p. 31), *sheath, escorted, scudded* (p. 32), *oath, filtered* (p. 33), *brazier, patrolled, pommel* (p. 34), *adversary, Roman Empire, unconscious* (p. 35).
- Help with the pronunciation of character and place names such as *Dubornos* (p. 21), *Brigantes* (p. 23), *Stanegate* (p. 24), *Flavian* (p. 25), *Housesteads Fort, Hadrian's Wall* (p.26).

Returning to the text

Develop children's understanding by asking some of these questions either during reading or at the end of the story. Encourage them to find the relevant part in the text to support their answers.

1) What is Dubornos plotting when he is overheard by Brean? (He is planning to "teach the Romans a lesson" by attacking the fort (p. 24).)
2) How does Dubornos behave when Centurion Marcus enters the inn? (He welcomes him and flatters him, but his welcome and flattery are false; even while the Centurion is present, he and the warriors are plotting their attack (pp. 24–25).)

3) What do you think Marcus means when he instructs his men to take Dubornos somewhere quiet and "rid us of him for ever" (p. 32)?)

Note how Dubornos addresses Brean as "Boy". What does this tell us about the way he regards his nephew? How does Centurion Marcus address Brean? (To begin with, he also uses "Boy", but at the end of the story he calls him "Landlord" (p. 36).)

Talk about the dilemma Brean faced. Reread the line on p. 28: "Much as he hated his uncle, no one betrayed their own people." What made him decide to betray his uncle? (Brean was treated badly by Dubornos whereas Centurion Marcus had shown him kindness. Brean also believed that if the warriors rebelled against the Romans, his own people would suffer (p. 28).) Do the group think Brean was right? Or should he have remained loyal to his uncle and his own people?

Discuss the punishments inflicted on Dubornos and his friends by Centurion Marcus. Did they deserve to die for their crimes?

Think about the way in which the author successfully evokes a sense of Roman Britain in this historical story. As well as entertaining the reader, the author gives a flavour of the period and what it was like to live under the occupation of another culture. The British warriors are "dark and threatening", their hair hangs "in a tangled, matted web" (p. 21). These untamed men are filled with violent intentions (p. 24). But they lack the organised approach of barrel-chested Centurion Marcus, who effectively quashes their rebellion.

Next steps

Children can complete Activity Sheet 2: "Where Does My Loyalty Lie?" which asks them to put themselves in Brean's shoes and write a diary account outlining his dilemma.

Where Does My Loyalty Lie?

Imagine you are Brean: should you warn Centurion Marcus about the attack on the Roman fort, or should you stay loyal to your uncle? Write a diary account describing the problem and expressing your thoughts and feelings.

Make notes about Centurion Marcus and Dubornos before you begin. Think about the way they behave and how they treat you.

Dubornos	Centurion Marcus
• Treats me unkindly	• Gave me a home
•	•
•	•
•	•

I couldn't sleep last night. I lay awake thinking about the conversation I overheard...

_____

_____

_____

_____

_____

_____

_____

_____

_____

White Wolves Teachers' Resource
for Guided Reading Year 6
Comparing Fiction Genres
© A & C Black 2008

Escape from the Workhouse:
Teaching Sequence 3

Teaching Sequence

Introduction
Find out if the group know what a workhouse is and the reasons people entered them. What sort of life might an orphaned child, living in Victorian Britain, find in such a place?

Independent reading
Ask the group to read aloud the story, focusing on reading for meaning.

- Discuss less familiar words and phrases such as *beadle, serge dress* (p. 39), *threadbare* (p. 40), *cholera, lurid* (p. 42), *cavernous, malnourished* (p. 44), *roster, assigning, cess toilets* (p. 45) *regimental fashion* (p. 46), *scabies, vermin, mouldering* (p. 47), *paupers, poor-law guardians, noble institution, scullery girl, dilly-dallying* (p. 49), *staggered, shilly-shallying, patrol, subdue* (p. 50), *wielded, cavalry sabre* (p. 52), *warren of slums, quayside, capstans, hauled, toil* (p. 56).
- James and Anne's father was a "keelman" (p. 42); explain that a keel is a barge for carrying coal on the River Tyne.

Returning to the text
Develop children's understanding by asking some of these questions either during reading or at the end of the story. Encourage them to find the relevant part in the text to support their answers.

1) How do James and Anne feel when they enter the workhouse? (They are frightened; Anne does not want to leave her brother's side (p. 39).)
2) What do you think James and Anne would have found most difficult about being in the workhouse? (For example, their separation from one another; only being able to communicate, through eye contact and small gestures.)
3) What do you think will happen to the children after their escape? Are they really free?

Talk about the strong opening line to this story: "The door of the workhouse banged shut behind them like the lid of a coffin" (p. 39). Does the group think the simile is effective? Ask them to look for another simile on the page ("The two children… shuffled through like frightened sheep") and discuss the way similes can enrich a story, giving the reader a deeper understanding of the characters' predicament.

Note the various terms used to describe children in the workhouse. For example: "daft lump" (p. 40), "lazy hounds" (p. 43), "human vermin" (p. 47), "stupid boy" (p. 51), "little monsters". Discuss how they tell us more about the cruel and merciless character of the beadle than the orphans he refers to.

Look at the descriptions of the food served in the workhouse, which add to the overall grim picture conveyed by the author throughout this historical story. For example: "a sticky mess" (p. 45); "a thin, brown liquid, which the beadle called soup. Floating on the surface, a few strange lumps, possibly meat … nudged against one another amongst silvery specks of grease." (dinner, p. 46); "an occasional cabbage leaf or mouldering piece of cheese…" (p. 47).

The group could hot-seat characters from the story and ask children role-playing the parts of James and Anne what life was like inside the workhouse and they could ask the beadle how he sees himself; what he thinks of the children in his care; whether he misses military life.

Next steps
Using Activity Sheet 3: "Beadle Rules and Regulations", children can write a list of workhouse rules, using formal language and drawing on the text for inspiration.

Beadle Rules and Regulations

Imagine you are the beadle at the workhouse. Write a list of the rules and regulations that you expect all children to adhere to – or else!

RULES

1. *Backs straight at all times, no slouching!*
2. *Whistling is strictly forbidden.*
3. _____
4. _____
5. _____
6. _____
7. _____
8. _____

Write a paragraph outlining your role and responsibilities.

As the beadle at this establishment, I have been appointed to keep order and ensure that discipline is observed at all times. My duties include…

_____
_____
_____
_____
_____
_____

White Wolves Teachers' Resource
for Guided Reading Year 6
Comparing Fiction Genres
© A & C Black 2008

Left Behind: Teaching Sequence 4

Teaching Sequence

Introduction
Explain that this story is set in France in 1940. Can the group tell you what was happening at this time? Pinpoint Belgium, France and the Channel on a map for the children to refer to during the story.

Independent reading
Ask the group to read aloud the story, focusing on reading for meaning.
- Discuss less familiar words and phrases such as *convoy*, *German Stuka dive-bombers*, *tailgates*, *dank* (p. 59), *plumes*, *evacuees* (p. 60), *Ypres*, *cemeteries* (p. 61), *detonated* (p. 63), *sergeant* (p. 64), *hoisted* (p. 65), *infantry*, *charges*, *barricaded* (p. 66), *ammunition* (p. 67), *interspersed*, *mortars* (p. 68), *juddered*, *spent shell cases*, *comrades* (p. 69), *artillery* (p. 70), *tarpaulin*, *throttle* (p. 71), *Dunkirk* (p. 74), *wreath* (p. 75), *remnants* (p. 76).
- Talk about the meaning of the colloquial terms *nippers* (p. 63), *saddled with* (p. 64), *Blighty* (p. 75).
- Help the group to pronounce and translate the French phrases: *"Qui sont"*, *"Excusez-moi, Mademoiselle"*, *"Nous sommes Anglais"*, *"Allez!"* (pp. 72–73).

Returning to the text
Develop children's understanding by asking some of these questions either during reading or at the end of the story. Encourage them to find the relevant part in the text to support their answers.
1) How did the boys come to be travelling through France? (They were trying to escape the German invasion and head for Britain (p. 61).)
2) What were the British soldiers doing? (They were trying to slow down the German advance while retreating to the French coast (p. 65).)
3) Why were Ernest and the boys stopped by French soldiers? (The French soldiers had created a roadblock and were to prevent any Germans from crossing the line (p. 72).)

Talk about the opening line: "Dive-bombers! Dive-bombers!". What do the group think about this attention-grabbing start? Did they know immediately what sort of story this would be?

Look at how the author has developed the story's setting. Ask the group to find effective descriptions, for example: **River:** *At the bottom of the slope, a dark, twisting ribbon of a river wrapped itself around a small village* (p. 62).

Point out the author's use of metaphor, simile and alliteration and see if the children are able to spot other examples.

Talk about the battle scenes at the heart of the story. How does the vocabulary differ from other fictional writing? Ask the group to find examples of the special language associated with warfare. For example; "Bren guns stuttered into action, interspersed with volleys of rifle fire. (p. 68); "Spent shell cases clinked and gleamed across the floor" (p. 69). Unlike other forms of writing, fiction can give a greater insight through rich detail and imagery. For example, the powerful images above help readers who haven't experienced warfare get a sense of how it might have felt to be in the thick of it.

Two of the children could pretend to be Reggie and Len, 60 years after the story takes place. The rest of the group could interview them about their experience, asking them how they felt at particular points in the story. What do they think of their rescuer? Did their wartime experience have an impact on the rest of their lives?

Next steps
Activity Sheet 4: "Back in Blighty" is an extension activity based on the children's role-play situation. From the perspective of Reggie or Len, children can write about their wartime experience and the actions of their rescuer.

Back in Blighty

Put yourself in the shoes of either Reggie or Len. Write a memoir about your wartime experiences and the heroic actions of your rescuer, Ernest Grisstock.

Think about how you felt when:

- the lorry drove off without you;
- you heard the explosion as the British soldiers blew up the bridge;
- you drove through the French blockade in a sidecar;
- you sailed across the Channel towards Britain.

What do you think about your rescuer?

Did your wartime experience have an impact on the rest of your life?

_____

_____

_____

_____

_____

_____

_____

_____

_____

_____

_____

_____

White Wolves Teachers' Resource
for Guided Reading Year 6
Comparing Fiction Genres
© A & C Black 2008

Comparing Fiction Genres:
less experienced readers

A Special Sort of Cat (ghost story)
The Sun God (historical story)
Alien Invasion! (sci-fi story)

Teaching Sequence

Introduction
Ask the children to spend a few minutes skim reading the stories again to remind themselves of the characters and setting.

Ask the group to give a brief synopsis of each of the stories. Are they able to summarise what happened in just a few sentences? Which of the three stories did they enjoy reading the most? Ask them to explain their preferences.

Returning to the text
Note the different features of each story that set them in a particular genre. For example:

A Special Sort of Cat: the shadowy cat that seems to appear from nowhere; the birthday candles that mysteriously relight themselves (p. 16); the "nice lady" tending the grave of her father who has been dead for over a hundred years (p. 21).

The Sun God: the ancient Egyptian setting; ancient customs are described, such as the preparation of the dead king's body for the afterlife (pp. 14 and 15).

Alien Invasion!: a flying saucer; terrifying "Krell" aliens with slimy white skin, staring yellow eyes and cruel red mouths (pp. 15–16); alien capability of repairing a flattened shed with a dazzling beam of light (p. 19).

Think about what might happen if characters from two different kinds of stories were to meet. For example, imagine what might happen if the family from *Alien Invasion!* were to visit the tomb of Tutankhamun while on holiday in Egypt and found themselves confronted by the ghost of Hamu.

Discuss how you could combine a sci-fi story with a historical story and create a ghost story. Explore the idea further through role-play; what would Hamu tell Megan and her family about his previous life as cupbearer to the god-king? How would Megan's parents and little brother, Lewis, react to the sight of a ghost?

Next steps
The children can look for words and phrases that help to establish the genre in extracts from different types of fiction using Activity Sheet 1: "A Special Sort of Language". Emphasise that the children are to seek examples of language that set each story apart from other types of fiction.

A Special Sort of Language

Each of these extracts is from a different type of story. Read each extract and write what sort of story it is. Underline the words and phrases that give clues to this.

The aliens stopped in front of them, one standing ahead of the others. He was slightly taller, and Megan assumed he was the leader.

"Surrender, Earthlings," he said in a harsh voice. "We are the Krell, and this planet is now ours. If you resist you will be... utterly destroyed!"

"Hey, steady on," said Dad. "There's no need to be so aggressive. You can't go around taking other people's planets and threatening them."

"Quite right," said Mum. "Apart from anything else, it's very rude."

"SILENCE!" roared the alien. "You will obey us or you will die. The rest of our fleet is in orbit round the planet and will be landing soon."

"Hey, I bet that's the cloud of meteorites I heard about on the news," said Lewis. "What a great disguise for an invasion fleet. This is so cool!"

Type of story: _____

As I turned to go, I saw Mina's emerald eyes glint in the sunlight. Out of the corner of my eye, I watched her shadow dissolve into a million rays of sunshine that danced over the grave. A warm glow spread through my heart.

Mum looked back. "Where did Mina disappear to?" she asked.

"I... I'm not sure," I said.

"Mina's gone back with the nice lady," Jack announced. He skipped happily down the path with Mum trotting after him.

I stayed behind for a moment, transfixed by the date on the gravestone. The same day and month as Dad's death... but the year... the year was 1900. How could that old lady remember a father who had been dead for more than a century? And how could a cat live that long?

Type of story: _____

My name is Hamu, son of Harum. I came to court as cupbearer to Tutankhamun. My duty was to make sure that if the king wanted wine, it would always be ready for him. My father had fought and died in the wars with great bravery. My family were poor and the king had given me this job so my mother would not starve.

We had lived in a simple house made of clay bricks. When I first entered the king's palace, I was amazed. I could not believe that humans could build such a place.

I was entering another world; one of giant pillars of stone. Walls shimmered with paintings of the gods in brilliant reds and blues. Rich nobles shone with golden jewellery. I gazed around me in astonishment.

Type of story: _____

White Wolves Teachers' Resource
for Guided Reading Year 6
Comparing Fiction Genres
© A & C Black 2008

Comparing Fiction Genres:
Independent readers

Seekers / Shadow Puppet
(ghost stories)

Dark Eagle / Escape from the Workhouse (historical stories)

This is Not Earth / Space Pirates (sci-fi stories)

Teaching Sequence

Introduction
Ask the children to spend a few minutes skim reading the stories again to remind themselves of the characters and setting.

Ask the group to give a brief summary of each of the stories they have read. Which of the three stories did they enjoy reading the most? Ask them to explain their preferences.

Returning to the text
How do the settings differ? Compare the familiar settings in the opening pages of the ghost stories with Planet K1754 in *This is Not Earth*, which has pink sky and purple sand (p. 23) and the hostile workhouse environment in *Escape from the Workhouse* where a "beadle" orders orphans around in military fashion (p. 44). Discuss the ways in which setting helps to establish the genre of the story.

Talk about the characters in the historical stories: Brean, James and Anne. Do they behave differently from characters in stories with modern settings? Discuss how they are treated by the adults around them. In both stories, the children are not addressed by name (Brean is referred to as "Boy"; James and Anne are referred to by number). In both stories there is the belief that it is acceptable to treat children cruelly. In *Escape from the Workhouse*, the children suffer at the hands of

the beadle; in *Dark Eagle*, Brean is treated cruelly by his uncle and, even Marcus is said to have "realised that boys needed a cuff now and then" (p. 27). These things tell the reader a great deal about the times in which the stories are set.

Think about the story *Seekers* and discuss how it combines elements of both historical fiction and ghost stories. Why do historical settings work well in ghost stories? What makes an old house feel spookier than a new house?

How do the authors use language to make their stories feel more authentic and believable? Ask the group to find examples of historical, ghostly and sci-fi language in each of the various books (each group member could focus on a different book). For example: "They shot past Rigel 3's moon and the other planets in the system, several of which were enormous gas giants, and whizzed through a belt of ice-bound asteroids" (*Space Pirates*, p. 45).

Next steps
The children could draw comparisons between two stories from different genres using Activity Sheet 2: "Comparing Different Stories".

Comparing Different Stories

Choose two stories from different genres, for example, a ghost story and a sci-fi story. Use this chart to help you compare the different features found in each.

Title		
Author		
Genre		
Type of story		
Setting		
Characters		
Special language used		
Summarise, in a couple of sentences, what sets each story apart from stories in other genres.		

Which of these stories did you enjoy most and why?

_____

_____

_____

_____

White Wolves Teachers' Resource
for Guided Reading Year 6
Comparing Fiction Genres
© A & C Black 2008

Comparing Fiction Genres:
More experienced readers

Smelling of Roses (ghost story)
Left Behind (historical story)
Everything I Need (sci-fi story)

Teaching Sequence

Introduction
Ask the children to spend a few minutes skim reading the stories again to remind themselves of the characters and setting.

Ask the group to give a brief summary of each of the three stories they have read. Which of the three stories did they enjoy reading the most? Ask them to explain their preferences.

Returning to the text
Consider the ways in which the different authors have used specific language and vocabulary to make their stories feel more authentic and believable. Ask the group to find examples. In *Left Behind*, for example, the author has used names that are characteristic of the period: Len, Reggie and Ernest. He has included references to wartime features such as dive-bombers, evacuees and the "grey lines of German infantry" (p. 66). On p. 62, the author states, "here they were... in 1940, at war again", leaving the reader in no doubt as to when this historical story is set.

Compare the landscapes in *Left Behind* and *Everything I Need*. One story is historical, the other is futuristic, and yet both feature landscapes that are similar in many ways; why is this?

Discuss how *Everything I Need* also features elements that are characteristic of ghost stories. For example: "The boy shivered, and looked up to see that the sun had gone behind a bank of dark-grey clouds. A chill wind swirled the dust round his boots, and he had a vision of himself walking down endless, empty streets for the rest of his life, the ruined houses on either side full of ghosts whispering his name, begging him to come and join them." (p. 76). Explain that stories aren't always limited to one particular genre; they often draw on elements of several types of fiction. Can the children think of other examples?

Talk about the story *Smelling of Roses*. Although it is a ghost story, the author has also drawn on elements of historical fiction as part of the story is set in the past. Think about the way in which the cotton mill links the past and the present in this story.

Next steps
Using Activity Sheet 3: "Change of Scene", children can rewrite an extract from the historical story *Left Behind* in the style of a ghost story or sci-fi story. Discuss what features they will change. For example, in a sci-fi version, the soldiers with rifles may become space marshals with laser guns; the meadow may become a desert landscape with craters and space rocks.

Change of Scene

Read this extract from *Left Behind*, a historical story set in 1940, and rewrite the scene in the style of a ghost story or a sci-fi story.

Consider:
- When your version will be set.
- Which features need changing.
- What new details will need adding.

Through the screen of trees, they could see the dark shapes of soldiers moving steadily towards them, rifles raised. Fear crushed their chests. They didn't know whether to shout or run for their lives. But it was no use running across an open meadow. They would be shot down before they'd covered a few desperate yards.

  Reggie pushed his brother down into the long grass. Their hearts were pounding. Their hands clenched till the knuckles went white. They dared not breathe. They could feel the soldiers getting closer through the whispering grass. A shadow loomed over them but they dared not turn over and face their enemy.

_____

_____

_____

_____

_____

_____

_____

_____

_____

_____

Record Card

Group:	**Book:**
Focus for Session:	

Name	Comments

The White Wolves Interview:
Tony Bradman

What sort of stories do you enjoy reading?
All kinds – historical, fantasy, realistic. I've always loved SF, though, and often find myself returning to it both as a reader and a writer.

Describe the place where you like to write.
A beautiful, futuristic house high on a crag overlooking a tumbling mountain river… on the planet Altair 3. But I'm usually to be found at my desk in my Earth-bound house. It faces a big window with a view out over the city, and sometimes it does feel as if I'm at the controls of a spaceship.

What do you think are the essential ingredients for a good sci-fi story?
It needs to be strange and give you a sense of wonder at what people and the universe might be capable of, but completely believable at the time. The best SF stories take things that might be possible and make them happen!

Why do you think fantasy and sci-fi stories are so popular with both children and adult readers?
It's that sense of wonder thing, the feeling that an amazing 'what if?' kind of question gets answered. What if I could travel in space or time? (How cool would that be?) What if there was a catastrophe and almost everyone in the world were killed? (And how terrifying would that be!)

The White Wolves Interview:
Neil Tonge

What sort of stories do you enjoy reading?
Well you may have guessed it by now –
historically-based stories. If I read a novel I like it
to be quirky, something odd about its structure or
the manner of writing. If it's history non-fiction,
then I like it to be detailed to show the historian
has done his research but without losing a good
grip on narrative.

Describe the place where you like to write.
I have a book-lined study – lined with history
books of course. I'm fortunate in living in
beautiful countryside and so views from the
window and walks stimulate thinking time.

**Is there a period in history that fascinates
you more than any other?**
History is not just a passion for me, it's an
obsession! So just about every historical period, in
whatever shape or form, fascinates me. However, if
I was put on the rack, I would confess to history at
either end of the spectrum – modern world history
and the Roman Empire.

**What sort of research do you carry out
before writing a story with a historical
setting?**
Well, you need to know that I was a history
teacher and advisor for over thirty years and I
devour history books like novels, so I have a
some knowledge of most historical periods.
However, I do like to soak myself in at least a
couple of detailed studies. Not too much when
I'm writing fiction, strangely enough, as you
can't allow too much detail to get in the way
of good storytelling.

The White Wolves Interview:
Jane Clarke

Describe the place where you like to write.
I like to write at the kitchen table, with a steaming cup of tea by my side and two snoring Labradors at my feet.

What do you enjoy doing when you are not reading or writing?
When I'm not reading or writing, I enjoy walking the dogs and hunting for fossils.

What do you think are the essential ingredients for a good ghost story?
A believable setting and main character (or characters) that the reader can identify with. A good or evil ghost of someone or something that once lived on earth and has a reason to be in the setting and meet that character. An atmosphere of spookiness and mystery that gradually builds up. An exciting moment when things go badly for the main character, or there's a twist or surprise in the tale. An ending that answers some questions, but leaves others unanswered.

What sort of stories do you enjoy reading?
I enjoy reading mystery and detective stories and trying to work out 'whodunit' before I'm told.

White Wolves Resources for Guided Reading

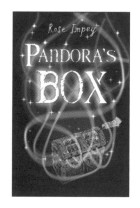

White Wolves Resources for Guided Reading

Year 4

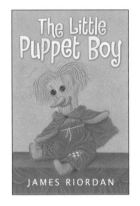

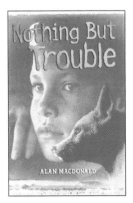

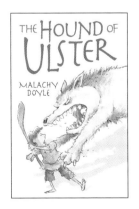

White Wolves Resources for Guided Reading

Year 5

Year 6

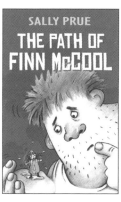

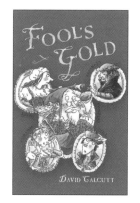

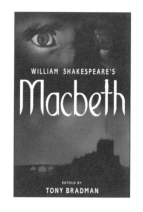

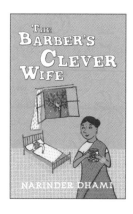

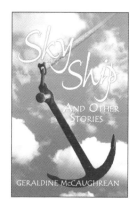

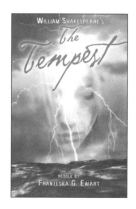